Emote

A Poetry Collection

JADE DIVAC

Dedication

To all the past versions of myself:
You were strong, even when you didn't think you were.
I've got you now.

Content Note

This collection explores the emotional
landscapes of love, longing, heartbreak,
and healing.

Some pieces include references to sexual
intimacy, non-consensual experiences,
depression, and the experience of loving
someone who is suicidal.

Please take care of yourself as you move
through these pages.

Humans are made for this —
to emote the feelings that come,
surround us,
overtake us,
leave us on our knees,
begging to be left alone.

They won't.
You've tried it all before,
as have I.
The pleas,
making deals,
turning voicemail on
as if emotions could be so easily tricked.

But we are humans,
and emotions belong to us,
as was intended.

So take charge,
but give in —
and let them flow through.

Emote.

Emotions

Sadness

Emote

Footsteps

The footsteps I hear
from my third-floor apartment are yours.
Haste drives them upwards, quicker and louder.
Desperation brings them to my door,
along with the regretful man who makes them.

With pride disheveled, you say
you were a fool, an idiot, so wrong.
That the man who deserves me is the man you'll become.
You'll be better – you'll prove it.
And mark your words:
you'll fight the world to have me
and show me your love.

The footsteps stop at the door opposite mine.
Keys jingle.
A door opens and shuts.
A neighbor is home with heavy groceries,
and you never came.

Someday

I do everything hoping:

Maybe someday he'll love me.
Maybe someday he'll love me.
Maybe someday he'll love me.

But I don't think he ever will.

Slant Love

I love you more than I can say,
though I tried
       word after word,
       line after line,
       stanza after stanza,
       poem after poem.

I bound them together,
every piece I wrote for you.
But you didn't read them all.

That green notebook,
a part of myself,
stayed for months on your desk.

I asked you why
because it hurt me so much.
Finally, you told me.

You said you couldn't finish because
they show how much I love you,
and you just don't feel the same.

(H)our Loss

I deleted your timezone
from my lock screen widget.
But its absence does nothing
to stop my mind
from automatically subtracting an hour
whenever I check the time.

I wish ours wasn't through.

Empty Roads

When all distractions have faded,
and the road lies empty before me,
my mind has no choice
but to run straight to you.

You occupy my thoughts,
overtake any silent serenity,
and although no longer mine,
leave me painfully full of you.

We Can't Always Have What We Wish

I'm going to miss the nicknames you gave me
when I add them to the graveyard of my love.
They may join one or two others,
never to grace my ears again.
Once laced with affection,
they'll never sound the same repeated.

I wish to hear them once or twice more
before they retire.
They lived so short a life.
But we can't always have what we wish.

(I may even wish they'd still live on from your very lips.
But we can't always have what we wish...)

Emote

The Love You Deserve Won't Come from Me

We sat together on a park bench,
my head on his shoulder
but face turned away.
Amidst silent, soft, slow-rolling tears,
I mustered out loud
a thought I've been trying to morph
from distress into comfort.

"Maybe love isn't supposed to come to me.
Pain is what fuels me.
Maybe love would silence my art."

And he said, "No.
You deserve love."

But what he didn't say was,
"I am going to hold your hand
and your face
and your heart.
But the love you deserve
won't come from me."

Unofficial Ex

How sad it is
to share tears,
laughs, pain, and joy
with someone.
To sleep in their arms
and be given kisses,
yet to not be able to label them
as once so special
because they were never willing
to label you as such —
even when asleep in their arms,
kiss imprints drying on your forehead.

Emote

To No Longer Know You

To revert to being strangers
is perhaps the hardest pill to swallow
when it comes to heartbreak.
How steep the decline is
from lovers to nothing at all.
From talking all day
to never speaking again.
From knowing each other's
lore, secrets, and vulnerable feelings,
to merely hoping they're doing well —
but sitting in the hurtful reality
that you only get to hope.
You'll never get to know.

Loaner

You're everything I wanted
and nothing I could keep.

Emote

Ex-Recipient

Good news — and you're the first I want to tell.
And you used to be.
Now I call my mom
and tell my roommate when she's home.
Your number is forbidden to me
because that song with Selena and Charlie Puth —
"We Don't Talk Anymore" —
that's what we're striving to be.
Trying to go forward, move on,
but I'm dying.
On the outside, I'm okay when my mind is busy,
but tonight I almost cried for joy —
and then I cried for real
because I couldn't share it with you.

When I Go Home

they'll tell me you're a douche,
although they'll probably just say jerk.
They'll talk you down to raise me up,
but it'll only sink me deeper.
I was committed to you
until you forced it from me.
But ties can't be severed with your lies.
Though I wish it were clean-cut,
and love could stop in its tracks,
do an about-face, and run far into the distance —
away from the hurt,
and away from the version of myself who loved you.

Emote

Good as New

Cut me deep —
make me bleed.
Sew me up,
but I still leak.

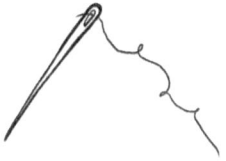

Backyard Burial

When that first pet dies,
and your parents are forced to tell you
of death and its concept,
your little brain will never consider it
anything other than
a tragedy and a theft,
and would never imagine
that someday you'll also have to learn
that some people want it,
and one of them might be someone you love.

Emote

Side Effect of Heartbreak

The one time I thought I would write
with words flowing endlessly from me,
I can't — they won't come.

I looked forward to this in a way —
as a promised event of inspiration.
But the sadness isn't that.

It's just sadness.

Workshop

I've thought perhaps you have broken wing syndrome.
I felt like a project.
Now I feel abandoned in your workshop.

Maybe you do have it.
Maybe my wing is just too broken
to make a worthwhile project.

Emote

The Legacy of Crazy

It's going to kill me
that your friends
will think I'm crazy
when I'm gone –
because you cannot hear me
no matter how many times,
in however many variations,
I say that I want you
and want you to know me.

They will think
I was just too much
(which you made me fear is true)
because I expressed a need
you had no desire to meet
so I could stay here
by your side.

They won't even know
how sad I am to go –
how much I wish you cared enough
to want to be the safe space
I need in someone.

A Love Lost

A love lost, to me, is a death.
Maybe I was less to you —
a blip in your year or your life.
But love holds weight to me,
and to release it,
drags me down further
before I can resurface.

In the span of a lifetime,
maybe we were a blip.
But how full,
how heavy the heart can grow
in only a sliver of time.
How jarring it can feel
to lose love's mass.

Emote

Szechuan Button

Isn't it strange
how you can dislike
a name,
but then one day
it starts to taste
like honey
in your mouth?

And isn't it strange
how you can love
a name,
and suddenly,
one day,
you never want
to hear
or murmur it again?

Love-Bruised

As the color slowly muted
from the stark yellow
of a healing mark,
I pressed a few fingers to it
on my chest,
near my heart,
and wept for you
and the disappearance of
this last piece I had of you
and of our lovely love.

Emote

Projected Outcomes

I've tested to see if
expecting the disappointment
makes it hurt any less.

The results are unsubstantiated.
What's the point of less?
It hurts regardless.

Despair

Emote

An Aggression of Color

How can the sunset be
so pink and pretty
when life is so dark and haunting?

Making Home

All I wanted was to get to the point
where loving you felt safe
and I could make a home in your arms.

Heavy Secret

A heavier secret has never existed
than being alone in knowing
that your loved one wants to die.

Astrophysics

You fell in love with science
long before you met me.

You grew an affinity for space
and the complexity of a universe
we can only partially conceptualize.

But studying space taught you that
in its vastness,
you are insignificant.

Maybe it's coincidental
that you especially love black holes,

since here you are,
wishing to be taken by a void –
to disappear
and forever cease existence.

But you are significant to me.

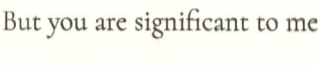

I hate physics.

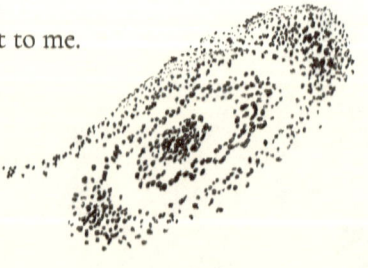

Living Bereavement

Even though you came home
instead of ending your life,
the moment I learned you don't want to live,
I slipped into grieving,
and I can't conceptualize how to leave it.

Not Just a Bystander

I know I'm not the victim
in you wanting to end your life.
But how does one process
the love of their life
hoping to die?

Emote

Aging

They told me I'd peak at 25,
but they never mentioned
I'd spend 27 wishing I was numb.

Love is Not a Medication

I just want to tell you I love you
until I burst.
Until it helps.
Until you are happy again.

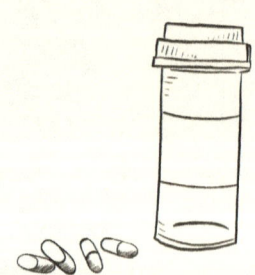

Emote

Wound Me

because I cannot spare myself the pain
of calling this what it is —
by saying we're through.
Break my heart for me
because I cannot break it myself.
Disillusion me
because I am high on your fantasy,
and in this state
(some call it love),
I must be destroyed
to release my hold on hope.

So destroy me.
Murder my heart in my chest.
Spare me of my own incapable hand.

The Hardest Thing

I've ever had to learn to date
is that I can't love hard enough
to fix things for you,
shoulder your pain,
or make you want to live.

Emote

Cracked

Your attraction is fading.
I'm so broken
that you're losing the vision
of how I could fit into your future.

I don't think I can blame you.
I hate all my cracks.
If love is water,
I'm letting it slip through.

All I want is wholeness,
and I can't wish it hard enough to have
right here
right now.

So let the attraction die.
You deserve better than broken.

Non-Participant

I wish that I could grab my heart
right out of my chest,
put it on a table in front of me,
and watch it contract and release,
puddling in its own goo
— and feel nothing.

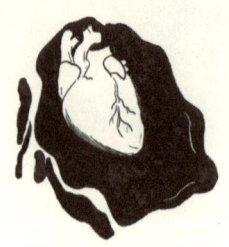

Emote

Close But Not Enough

You were always a little out of reach.
Maybe it was by design.
Perhaps programmed by the wounds
that search relentlessly
for people who will reopen them
just as I feel like I'm healing.
Were you self-punishment?
The tease of finding Mr. Almost Right —
yet not emotionally available?
A pressure to the bruise I wear
of not being enough for someone?

Close but not enough.
Close but not enough.
Close but now too broken —
therefore not enough.

I was never going to be it for you.
The reach was just too far.

Folklore

If you go early,
I hope like no other
that Heaven and Hell are folklore
and you get the eternal sleep
and empty void
you're thirsting for.

Anticipation

Emote

Subliminal

Did you get the message I sent
to the whole world,
addressed only to you?

Hurricane Watch

Being with you
was like
being under a hurricane watch.

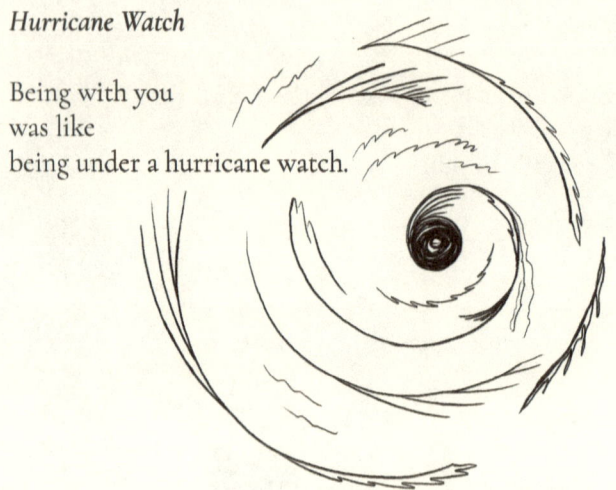

Emote

Sailors Take Warning

If bad luck is real,
you were a red morning sky.
I tried to weather your storms,
angry words pelting my umbrella,
your triggers causing natural phenomena.

Time Bomb

How long?
For how long?
Who even holds the pin
to our time bomb?
I'm terrified it's you,
but I'm terrified it's me.
How long until it blows?
— And who pulls the pin?

Weak

Are you going to break my heart
or are you going to break me down?
Use my love against me since I'm weak —
weak for love,
weak for you.
Too weak to see the truth.
Too weak to stand my ground.
Too weak to cause you pain.

Break my heart, don't break me down.
Otherwise, I'll let you.

Scar Tissue

We're so scared
that it's almost a goal
to find a flaw with the other
or in the concept of us.

It's protection.
It's survival.
It's been so long since either of us
felt safe enough to drop our guard.

We've lived lessons that hurt.
It scarred us —
by different weapons perhaps,
but scar tissue was created either way.

If I retract and cut myself,
and if you do the same,
it's almost less painful
than hoping it won't happen
and being proved wrong.

I know I don't want to give you scars.
I want to massage the ones
you already own.
You say the same.
But we haven't believed each other safe.

Emote

It's like the longer my arm is exposed,
and the longer I'm not healing a new scar,
the more afraid I am
that it will still come
and it'll be an even deeper cut.

How do we want the same thing
but we won't take it?
How can we change this
so that we don't have to lose our chance
to be safe for each other?

Gun Control

He said he's been like me —
in the place I am now,
after loving more than being loved.

So why did he do it to me?
Why did he protect himself
and make me take the fall?

I was made the victim
when he took out his gun.
Wounded himself, he shot me.

If I ever stand up again,
do I get myself a weapon
to protect my bleeding heart?

Do I keep it concealed
but leave the safeguard off,
having learned my lesson from love?

Wounded myself,
when love finally finds me,
do I raise my gun and shoot?

Emote

Don't Come for Me

I'm scared.
Small dollops of salted water
have been visiting without reason.
I sit here in tears and fear,
wondering if depression has come for me
because I don't know why I'm sad or energy-less —
why a new day doesn't excite me like it should.
I've seen what it can do —
blanket one in darkness with a fog too thick
to care to see through.
And I worry that if it comes,
I won't be a match.
That it'll swallow me, and I'll never again know
what it was like to love life
and the mystery of tomorrow.

Apathy

What I think will hurt the most
when we come to an end
is that I'll cry and have
the worst time mourning you,
and you'll most likely walk away,
dry-eyed and straight-faced.

And that's what will kill me.

Emote

Terminal

I know my heart's decaying,
but I'm still afraid of the poison.
Chronic pain feels more comforting
than sudden death's infliction.
Both will hurt me.
Both will kill me.
But I want my heart to live,
so I choose slow —
hoping there will come a cure,
but knowing that I'm headed for the grave
— because it's terminal now.

One Hundred to One

If you needed a reason to stay,
I'd have a hundred.
If I asked you the same,
would you even give one?

Emote

Waiting to Become a Whisper

I miss you already,
as I wait for you to confirm
that you aren't choosing me.
I mourn you already,
knowing that an extra dose of silence
waits to greet me each day,
and the withdrawal of your voice
is a symptom only time dilutes.

I both need your final answer
and hope it never comes.
I don't define myself by you
or need you to be whole,
but I've enjoyed you.
You've been a happiness
that has wrapped me up
in effortless affection
I'd never known
yet always dreamed to hold.

You are a wish waiting to become a whisper.
A dream I can't so easily awaken from
or forget.

Have I Lingered

How quickly did you remove my polaroid
from your wallet
when you decided that —
although you liked me enough to place it there —
you didn't like me enough to keep me around?

How soon did I leave the dreams
I used to visit you in at night?

Have your lips already forgotten my taste?
Has your cock forgotten how I made it twitch?

Has our intimacy and experience
already been shelved,
categorized,
forgotten,
gathering dust in the back of your mind?

Have I lingered?
Or am I already gone?

Emote

Screaming Silence

My alone time is invaded by you,
as the silence screams of your absence
and there's nothing I can do to shut it up.

Fear

Emote

Snapshot of a Smile

I didn't realize when I learned your name
or saw my first snapshot of your smile
that you'd find yourself at home in my poetry.

Maybe I should have warned you of the chance.
But, hi, welcome.

I'm torn that you're here
because here is caused by feelings,
and when I embarked to learn more of you
than your name and your smile,
I might have hoped we'd get here,
but I forgot to fear it too.

I only write confessionals.
This is my confession to you.

Love Stats

I have more experience loving
than being loved.
And while others may not know my score,
I do.
I fear the way it charts.
I fear collecting even one more data point
that makes me plottable.

I'm looking for an outlier.

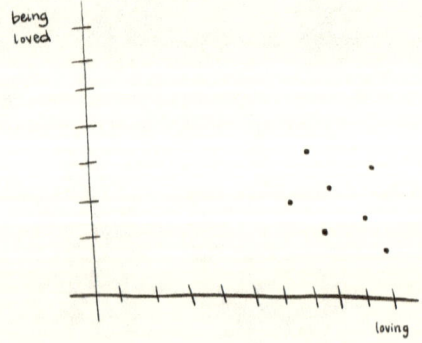

Emote

Spray Paint

Write of your love for me
on my soul with words,
on my body with marks,
on the town water tower with spray paint.
And maybe then
I'll start considering
it could be true.

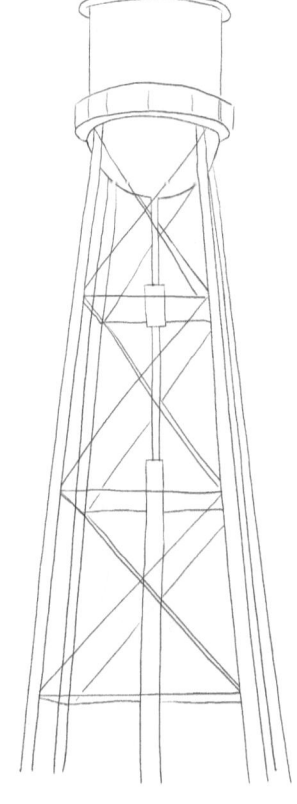

Emote

How Could I Have Gotten it So Wrong

Is it guilt that has bound you to me
through the years
instead of the love and passion
that I thought
were fueling my dream
and sealing my fate?

Cave Walls

I don't necessarily believe in fate,
but I have fears
that run along my mind like a frieze,
carving images of being alone,
unloved,
unlucky.

I've tried to hide it in the deep recesses
of my mind,
but I can't forget the path which leads me back,
an audience viewing art,
whenever it seems that my fears may be realized
and maybe I'm one step closer
to what's fated or
to a fear I'll self-fulfill.

If it isn't Love, I Don't Want it

Did you replace love with obligation
at some point along the way,
comfortable enough with leaving me
pining over someone
I thought truly cared?

Emote

Fire Dance

You act as if I never wanted to love you.
But I only wanted to love you.

Inconsistencies in my attachment
were not a reflection of not wanting to be attached,
but a fear of it —
a fire dance of a war within,
where Terror sliced down Desire
every time she came up for air.

It was a reflection of your own fire dance.
The war within you too afraid to love,
too afraid to be able to gift me peace.

If we had joined forces,
Desire could have won.
But we raged on
and gave Terror the upper hand.

Trip Hazard

Don't fall in love.

Love is a choice.
Falling means you fell,
and he might not care to catch you.

Emote

Gluttons

I feel like I'm offering myself like a meal,
going down the line of potentials,
asking each,
"Could you care enough for me
to not take a bite?"
But each does,
and I go on to the next,
determined to find the odd one out.

But I'm worried by my strategy —
there are only so many bites
that can be taken.
What if when I find what I'm looking for,
there's nothing of me left?

The Risk

What I said when in pain
as a buy-in to get through it was,
"If I love like this,
someone else must too."

But now I'm faced again
with maybe falling in love,
and I'm realizing my hope
is coupled with fear.

Because what if he's not one of them,
and I only think he might be?
What if, even if less malicious than the last,
this ends in heartbreak too?

Most of me wants to play the risk
because I know I won't find love
without baiting with my own.
But I'm still so tired.
I'm still holding so much trauma.

Emote

I truly fear having to,
any time soon,
spend more nights on my floor in tears,
picking myself back up
and spoon-feeding myself the lines
that this doesn't mean
there's anything wrong with me
or that I don't deserve love.

Disgust

Comforting Chaos

You taunted me with
what I've always wanted:
Pet names.
Affection.
Hope.

And another serving of the lesson
I refuse to ace:
that comforting chaos
is still chaos all the same.

Wine Drunk

I said I'd leave you be,
but I couldn't account for
being wine drunk
and getting called your moon again.

Emote

Motions

Towards the end,
I want you to know
we only fucked out of obligation.

Sex lives are linked with love lives,
and I thought putting out
could fix our love.

But the moments
of hardly keeping our hands off each other
were done —
replaced with a dim smile,
silent impatience,
and sedated volatility.

I should have listened to my body —
it knew to give up
before my mind would rationalize it.

Wounds

If you could see my inner wounds
as easily as outer wounds,
you wouldn't ask me
why I'm still in pain.

Even when wounds close,
scars replace them.

You can look at them
and remember your resilience.
But you can't remember your strength
without reliving your pain.

Wounded or scarred,
I hurt.

Emote

Filtered Truth

The truth is:
I put my love life on hold
because I wanted my love to be you.

Despite you saying you weren't ready,
despite you warning you didn't know when,
you said you wanted me.
That it would be nice to hold me.
And maybe someday would be our day.
— Just not today.

And so I dismissed the warnings.
I filtered out "maybe" and "someday."
I filtered in "I want you."

So maybe I'm the only one to blame
for my heartbreak.

Someday never came.

To Be Loved

Why does it always seem like I'm not enough,
even though I know I am?
Even though I know the love I hold
is transformative.
Enlightening.
Elative.

Maybe they don't want to be transformed.
They don't want to be enlightened
or elated.

Happy to choke on the returns of dealt chaos.
Then there'll be no fear that they're not deserving
of being loved
and seen
and known.

To be loved wholeheartedly is too terrifying,
and so to find someone to volunteer —
maybe it's just too hard.

Anger

Emote

Low Grade Men

I've only ever written these
for men
who didn't deserve my love —
much less
for men who deserved lines,
inked red
with the fluid of
my bleeding heart.

Roses Have Thorns

How did you pluck a rose
and act surprised by its prick to your skin?

Did you think something scented so sweetly
would be yours at no cost?

That there'd be no effort in harvesting
something that beautiful?

What reward is there in a challenge too easy?
What pat on the back should you receive
after winning such a stunning non-victory?

They say dopamine without effort
makes the brain weaker.
It's the effort that makes it stronger.

It is so with roses.
It is so with women.

If you don't like the thorns,
prune them.

Emote

Gallery Art

I can't believe I've once again
broken my own heart
by pouring into a man
who cannot love me like
the sweet and true goddess I am.

RIP to me,
but RIP to you,
for touching artwork
you can't afford to rehang

Emote

Know your Audience

You must not have known your audience
when you told a poet not to cry.

Ask me to ice over,
and I've frozen solid the very muse
that sings to my soul.

If my feelings are not safe with you,
I fear that you aren't my audience.

Emote

A Monster I Couldn't See

Maybe you were a type of monster
everyone but me could see,
with your worst parts exposed to
the one who'd only ever make excuses.

In the daylight, you'd slap me,
and I'd beg a ceasefire.
— Not for me,
but so others didn't see you as a monster,
since I couldn't see your claws.

In the moonlight —
or morning light —
or any time you wanted me,
you'd lure me in with safety
but expose yourself in me,
somehow believing I wouldn't feel the difference.
That I couldn't tell
you'd stripped the safety net away,
discreetly.

I didn't see you as a monster still.

Instead, I asked you to stop each time.
I begged it to never be done again.

Emote

When my requests didn't work,
I tried to be cunning,
asking which names you'd pick out —
despairing attempts to maybe
scare respect into you.

When scare tactics didn't work,
I simply gave up.
Did away with asking all together.
Learned not to expect safety as an element
in our physicality.

And you weren't a monster to me.

When we broke up eventually,
I mourned you.
Mad, even, that you were gone.

It wasn't until
I had my hands wrapped up
in a good man's
that I finally understood it when he told me
that is what a monster does.

Emote

Yet even with an excavation,
it doesn't feel all too different
here in the future.
I think maybe it should.

Because I could never see
the monster in you,
and because maybe I couldn't see
the victim in me,
I'm not angry.

But he's angry for me.
And I love him for that.

I Let You Poison Me

I let you poison me — can't play the full victim.
I saw the flags — I should have stopped.
But kind hearts, when not blind, play dumb,
and I was dumb to keep loving you.

I cried when you yelled, but I stayed with I'm sorrys,
yet most times I was the apologizer.
I'm sorry for making you mad.
I'm sorry — I didn't mean it that way.
I'm sorry — I should have realized.
I should have called first.
I should have stayed quiet.
I should have said something.
I should have known what you're thinking
or feeling
or that you have a headache
or that you got rained on when you walked home from the library.

No.
I'm sorry I stayed.
I'm sorry I apologized —
that I let you believe it was all on me —
that you were the victim.
I'm sorry I let you poison me.

Emote

Sorry I Led You On

I never got to hear the words
I thought you'd say my whole life.
I saw them in your eyes through stares,
laced with pure delight.
I felt them in the arms that wrapped me up
each tender night.
I heard them in the way we talked,
our futures unclear but bright.

We talked of moving in,
of rent and travels and families.
We spoke of marriage three years down,
a place, a pet, financials.
We discussed future children's religion
and argued over spanking...

And then it was gone.
"Sorry I led you on —
I hope you're not upset."

Tomorrow

I love that you see my potential
when you look at me,
seeing the capacity I have
for elevation of self.

You pushed me,
the push so gentle,
but the pressure so high
I pale in comparison
to who I could be.

I'll be there one day,
but this day is here now.

You'll love me tomorrow,
but I'm Annie today.

Emote

Hungover

You gave me every gift but you:
Time
Flowers
A quill
The excitement of the prospect of your love
        — enough to make my heart drunk.
But never you.

I'm hungover.

Regrets

You don't regret setting the moon free,
but do you regret not loving her enough
that her place in the sky
was exactly where she should be?

Emote

How Many More

How many more heartbreaks
        until I meet my peace?

Longing

Distance

The world is so big,
which is beautiful,
but I'm so far from you
that it's hell.

Hold Witness

What makes you not ready
to accept me and my love?

Do you think that,
as such an imperfect human myself,
it would startle me to learn you're the same?

Do you take me for a collector of benefits
when it would soothe me
to be loved by someone growing?
When it would invigorate my soul
to tackle life's challenges together?

Do you wish to be healed before you come to me
so that I may be the only party struggling
between the two of us?

We could both hold witness to each other,
radiating even more over time.

And as two people who want little more
than for the other to come into their light,
how silly it would be for us to miss the show.

Emote

I Wish

telling you
I love you
made you happy,
not scared.

(Dis)Comfort

At the end of the day,
after the harsh bearing of our souls,
I still want to tell him I love him
and have those words bring comfort,
though they never have yet.

Emote

Please Requite

Someday
maybe
you'll reciprocate
the love
in
my heart
for
you.

I hope that day is soon.

Chaos

I throw my noise into the crashes of the ocean,
hoping that amidst the chaos,
my sounds will travel to your ears.

Secret Messages

I long again to say, "I love you,"
but I'm still afraid.
So I say it in another language while you sleep.
I trace the words on your skin
while your subconscious is in control.
I look at you with love in my eyes,
hoping from them you'll understand.
I can't bear the vulnerability of confessing once more,
not knowing if enough has changed.
I talk myself away from the topic of you loving me every day.
I am so stricken in the heart.
I can't keep hands or lips from your body.
I love you.
I want so badly to remind you —
even more so to have it in return.

Emote

Warm Front

Something is different.
I can see it in your eyes.
I can feel it in your touch,
hands around me
and lips crashing against mine,
like waves from the ocean onto the shore.
I see your smile as you caress me.
You gift forehead kisses
and hold my hand.

Could this be
you finally loving me?

Emote

Inevitable

Knowing goodbye was coming
didn't make our kisses last any longer,
even though I thought maybe it could.
Even though I tried to cherish every moment,
they still slipped away.
I'm still here, in the future,
wishing I could stay
in those moments with you forever.

Emote

Don't You Remember?

Did you forget what it felt like when we first met
and stripped down to our thoughts and wants
with bared minds?

Don't you remember feeling the spark
that not only fused our connection,
but lit a fear of it too?

How scary it was to burn so hot for each other
so fast, yet so confidently?

We didn't know much, but we knew what we wanted,
The hunger was stronger than the stakes.

We've loved in every way possible,
with minds, bodies, and emotions.
I love you still as in the beginning — even more.
My world looks more fulfilling with you in it.

Tell me if you forgot what it felt like.
Tell me if you love me still — as in the beginning.
Tell me if your world has room in it for me too.

Emote

Timezones

You think you weren't enough for me,
but the loss of what could be
I carry on my back
across a world of timezones.
I think of you as you sleep
and dream of you while awake.

Hopefuls

We used to be lovers;
now we're just hopefuls.

Emote

To Move On

I almost mourn the day I wake up
and you don't cross my mind.

More recently than not, I got to hold you.
Kiss you.
Touch you.
Love you.

Now I sit with a pit in my abdomen,
knowing I'll never again get to hold you.
Kiss you.
Touch you.
Love you.

And I want to move on.
Of course, you want to be able to move forward
after reckoning with incompatibility.

And I know the day will come
when the thought of you
doesn't tighten my chest any longer.

But missing you keeps you with me.
It's almost like —
in some very distant way —
I can still kind of hold you.

Gravestone

A gravestone would be friendlier —
smooth, cold stone to touch and see.
Put to bed the ghost of you and me.

But my love lives on,
and I'm haunted by
what-if-we-had-gotten-through-this.

Emote

Feeding the Muse

I'm tired of thanking men for,
if nothing else,
feeding my muse.

I wanted to be the inspiration
this time around.

I want to ignite
a fire in the eyes
and a bubble in the gut.

I want to be the reason
someone else's heart swells.
The name that pops up
that makes them smile too wide
to hide from nosy bystanders.

I could cause emotions
that can't stay inside just the heart.
Something that has to come out
and comes out as art.

But I'm the writer.
Not the muse.
And I'll always be a writer,
but I really did also want to be the muse.

Real Estate

You felt like home.
— But a home I didn't fully feel safe in.
I'm just searching for real estate
where when I wake up in the morning,
my heart is just as I left it
when I laid down the night before.

Emote

Smile Lines

Give me smile lines,
and make them deep
so that when my body ages,
it will always read of our love.

Love Languages

If you wrap up a gift for me,
let it be safety.

Encircle me in your arms
and protect me.

Whisper in my ear,
"you're safe here."
And mean it.

Have my back
when others don't.

Never leave me
when I need you most.

Emote

Until Lovers Sleep

I just want to lay my head on your shoulder
and be in your arms, forgetting everything,
the sound of your heart keeping me with you.

I want to have my hands folded in yours
and your bright eyes focused on mine,
our words intermingled and our legs intertwined.

I want to stay there, comfortably happy,
pulses slowing and breath regaining
until we melt into a lovers' sleep together.

Promises

There is no certainty.
No cheat sheet to life
or love
or us.

Any promises we make to one another
are feathers in the wind,
contingent on a future.
I don't know if we will see all of them fulfilled
or half
or a quarter.

I know there are no promises
that our future lives on.
I don't have certainty,
but I have hope.

Devotion

Emote

One Taste

One taste of you
and a hundred poems
are conceived.

What I Know

I don't know yet if I love you.
But what I do know
is that I love the taste of your name
and the sound of your voice.
I love the weight of your hand in mine
and the pressure of your body pressed to mine.
I love the joy in your laugh
and the passion visible through your eyes.
I love the way you fit me into your arms,
and I love the dream
that we could spend our days together
until there are none left to spend.

Emote

But Then

I didn't think I could be
any more attracted to your eyes,
but then
you looked at me
with love in them.

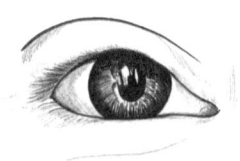

Body Language

I think there may be fewer things
I love more
than the intimacy of a simple hand hold.
To fit ourselves together in a touch
that can mean so many things:

I'm here
I love you
You're mine
I'll keep you safe
I need you
I want you
You're on my mind
I live for your touch

Emote

Skin

My skin loves yours.
My cold fingers drag over your chest,
silently memorizing the lines of your body,
hoping to never spend a night outside your arms,
where I am at home.
Your warmth encompasses me;
I know no fear with you.
Your hands in my hair,
drying kiss imprints collect on my forehead.
— This is love.
I don't have to question it.
Your eyes give you away.
The smile that pulls your lips upward as you stare
speaks the wordless truth.
It's all I can do to not speak it for you.
But it's there. It's there.
It's never more than a thought away,
and I'm never more than a second unhappy.
My being loves yours.

Safety Net

I asked,
"What if I fall?"

He said,
"I will catch you every time."

And I think that healed something within me
that had never not been broken.

My Ink is Made From Tears

My poetry's no good with love —
it always peaks with pain.
You're crippling my muse by loving me
wholly, fully, without restraint.

I don't know how to receive love,
non-toxic, healthy, and pure,
and still be able to pen my words.
My poems belong to pain and fear.
My ink is made from tears.

Keep my Heart

I was never skilled at picking a good man to love.
But for each, I fell and served my heart,
then picked it back up down the road.

You were the man I would have never met
in different circumstances.
But our minds connected over black holes and aeroplanes,
and our beings felt merged before even merging.

You were scary.
The way I felt — it was a terrifying rush of peace and passion.
You felt it too, which was worlds scarier.
I never expected something right to be so threatening.

But we fell, you and I, and we did it together.
We traded our hearts with a kiss.
Things have been hard here and there,
but we've done it this long, and I can say that I do
love you as much as ever
and carry that very same peace.

Keep my heart, my love.
It truly is for you.

Emote

Inconsequential

After realizing you are my home,
I came to also realize:

In any form you could take,
I will love you.
Through any ailment,
loss,
or identity-change,
you are mine.
My love isn't something so frail
that it could unravel
the moment you're no longer
young,
handsome,
able-bodied,
or male.

In all things and amidst all things,
my sexuality is you.

Irrelevancies

I could never know
what other timelines hold.
But what I do know
is that
I touch this one,
and you touch me,
and I'll never care to wonder.

Emote

Awakening

You make me a better person, my love,
not in morals, but in living.
I feel as if I was sleeping before,
and being awake is much more thrilling.

Resilience

Emote

I Needed ~~You~~ to Lose You

We want to, but we can't
— or won't —
give each other what we need.
Or maybe we can,
but not at the expense of denying ourselves our needs.

So, we won't give each other what we need.
We're forced to part and give unto ourselves,
wishing it was different.
That our needs didn't battle
That loss wasn't eminent.
That we didn't have to lose each other.

To lose you is hard.
To stop wishing for a different outcome:
               harder.
But one day we'll both be happy.
And today we should be proud
that we didn't lose ourselves to the other.

Find What You Need

I wish you only the best
out of life and love.
Find what you need
so that I can one day see
that this was always how
it was supposed to be.

Emote

Limbo is a Place

The love I want to capture,
the muse I want to fuel my poetry,
is not mine to have yet.

One day, the love I want
will come to me –
and I'll need to do nothing more
than welcome it.

My muse will show
when my writing
is ready to change tone.

To heavily anticipate another subject
would be to risk losing
what materializes in between.

Now is a time too.
Limbo is a place.
Confusion and healing
are muses just the same.

All poems shouldn't sing
the same melodies.

Chains of Control

I've spent so much time
trying to force myself to fit expectations
that don't complement my best self.

I've given so much emotional toil
to make a vision a reality
because I'm into someone.

I've tried to control my life far too much
that I've only succeeded in chaining myself
to those who cannot love me truest.

All these tears ago, I could have learned this
and saved myself so much tightness in my chest.

Everything that is meant for me will find me
and will stay by my imperfect side.
And everything that isn't will fade,
no matter the effort given.

I would rather let life give to me what it intends
because I cannot choose best.
And what a pressure lifted
to not be the author of my own fate.

Emote

Focus

Where are you hiding, my love?
For all this time I have been ready,
now I am not.
I'm growing to be a good person for you,
but now more than ever,
I'm growing for myself.

Since the concept of love was introduced,
you've been my focus —
my evading but passionate dream.
From that quest I now find myself broken,
with both new wounds and ones never healed.

I'm growing strong, but I'm doing my time,
loving, failing, rebuilding again.
Now more broken than ever,
I'm more focused as well.
But forgive me, my love —
right now I'm focused on myself.

Barbed Wire

The barbed wire that cuts you cuts me too
each time you reach out and touch what I had to create
to keep myself as whole as I can be
from day to day.
So that I don't have to suffer...
except on a random Tuesday because you wanted to reach out
when I've already told you I have to protect myself.

I didn't want to build this fence.
The distance between us kills me passively.
But I couldn't afford to keep dying actively.

Detoxing

Remember —
Heartbreak is a cleansing.
A detoxing of love not for you
so you can ready yourself
for the love that is.

Heartbreak is a Poet's Feast

Go ahead and break my heart;
it fuels my song.

Emote

Make More Noise

I know you hate when I cry,
but I will continue
because I can't let myself become
as icy as I'd need to be
to freeze each tear to bottle.

You wish for me to silence my emotions
so that they're easier for you to dismiss.

I won't.
I digest them aloud.
I sit with big feelings as they come.
I won't dismiss myself.
I am allowed to make noise in this world.

Maybe you should make more.

Imperfect Worth

How does it happen that
when I finally know how much I offer,
I feel like I've never been harder to love?

I've never had so much work before me,
but I've also never been more sure
that I'm worth each of my imperfections
and the growing pains of my healing undertaking.

Emote

Fisher

Your expectations are always taller
than I can reach,
and now my soul is tired
from stretching myself
into someone I wasn't.
For years I bit the line
that you threw out and reeled in
with your hopes and desires of
what I could love and want and do and dream.
But I've found myself now, recently,
and I'm no longer a fish on your hook.
I'm the fisher of my own destiny,
and there's only room on the dock for one.

Tired

If you ask me if I am tired,
I will say yes.
I am so tired.

I am tired of feeling
and being broken down by emotions.

I know feelings are what mean I'm alive.
I know hard things make me stronger.
I know they are my path.

But I think emotions can be my destiny
while wearing me out.

It's not every day when I want to feel resilient
or conversely — feel weak.

Some days I just want to get into bed
and tuck the covers up,
right under my chin,
like an invisibility cloak.
Like blood over my doorway,
begging feelings:

Emote

"Please pass over."
"Let me rest."
"Today I don't want to feel" —
or "I want to feel less."

But sadly,
you can't stop a heart in the chest
and escape death.

Ghost Kisses

I kissed a ghost yesterday —
a ghost of a love gone away.
I kissed him,
held him close,
listened to the memories
as they swirled around,
dancing on my skin.

I held him close,
and he begged me to stay
— there with him forever,
infatuated with the whispers
of everything we created together,
dancing on promises and dreams.

I kissed my ghost.
I held him.
And then I pulled away.
I wished him well.
I wished him freedom.
And then I turned,
and went to meet mine.

What I Hope for You

To those who have faced war not overseas, but on the home front, their bodies as the battlefield and someone forceful as the enemy:

I hope you find someone who loves you slowly and gently and wholly.
I hope you find the right person to trust, the right person to make you feel safe.
I hope you find someone patient and understanding, who knows damaged doesn't mean destroyed and broken doesn't mean unfixable.
I hope you find someone who makes you want to live again and love again and who puts vibrant happiness in your soul.

I hope you find that person and that you believe you will find that person.
And when you do, I hope you believe you are worth everything that person wants to give you.

When It Feels Like Too Much

Some of the pieces in this book hold grief, trauma, and the ache of survival. If anything you read stirred something too heavy to carry alone, please know there are people who want to help.

You are not alone, even when it feels like it.

Here are some places you can turn to:

For U.S. Readers

- 988 Suicide & Crisis Lifeline:
  Call or text 988
- RAINN (for sexual assault support):
  1-800-656-HOPE (4673)
- Crisis Text Line:
  Text HOME to 741741

For International Readers

- A list of global mental health hotlines is available at opencounseling.com/suicide-hotlines

Please take care of your heart. The world is more beautiful with you in it.

Meet The Poet

Jade Divac is a confessional free verse poet. She writes wherever she wanders, capturing the quiet truths we often carry but may not speak aloud.

Her work is shaped by heartbreak, healing, and the raw honesty of being fully human. She invites readers to feel without apology. To sit with sorrow, longing, and love, and to hold each emotion with gentleness before letting go.

She finds comfort in the hum of airports and the chaos of movement, often scribbling poems on planes and in places she's never been before. She often holds a passport in one hand and her heart cracked open in the other.

She uses poetry to process and honor emotions, especially the messy ones. She believes that when we gather the strength to speak from our softest places, we give others encouragement to do the same.

Follow the Writer

For more poetry, book updates,
and glimpses behind the pages
– follow @jadedivac
www.jadedivac.com

More to Come from Jade Divac

You Are Not The Man I Loved

If Emote was a whisper, this is a scream.
I survived the shattering,
but now I'm standing in the glass.

Bed Sheets & Moonbeams

Erotica with a pulse. Poetry with a bite.
Pleasure written like scripture
for those who long to be wrecked and
revered.

Acknowledgments

To my artist, Erica Prasad — thank you for lending your artistic talent to bring an extra dimension to my words. Thank you for creating something beautiful with me.

To my editor, Vanessa Dremé — thank you for your critique, candor, and for your belief in this project. Thank you for journeying with me through each iteration of this collection, from the first draft to the last.

To the team behind the scenes, my publishing consultant and my designer — thank you for lending your technical expertise to bring *Emote* to life.

To my village, the friends and family who read, critiqued, and lifted me up every step of the way — your support, in myself and in my art, is something I will never take for granted. The more you have believed in me, the more I have believed in myself. Each time I'm referred to as a poet as my identifier, it brings tears to the eyes of the little girl inside me.

And to the men who broke my heart — thank you (I guess).

To the Reader

You picking up *Emote* means the world to me.

This collection spans more than a decade of my life. Pieces from my first heartbreak live alongside pieces from my most recent. Everyone I have loved has made their way into these pages, and there are so many versions of myself in them as well.

Looking back through everything I've ever written, I caught glimpses of myself in my poetry that broke my heart for each younger version of me begging to be loved — and for the present me who still sometimes does.

Feeling is terribly heavy. We rarely offer ourselves grace, but it really is our first time living.

I have stepped into and shed so many versions of myself through writing these pieces and cultivating *Emote*. I am so proud to have it exist — and that you're holding it in your hands right now.

If something in my poetry resonated with you, I would be so appreciative if you shared your thoughts in a review on Amazon, Goodreads, or anywhere you feel moved to.

With heartfelt gratitude, thank you for supporting my art.

Emote

Copyright 2025 by **Elizabeth Erhartic**.

Written by **Jade Divac**

www.jadedivac.com
@jadedivac
jadedivac@gmail.com

Cover art and interior illustrations by **Erica Prasad**

www.ericaprasad.com
@ericaprasadart
ericaprasad@gmail.com

Cover design and internal formatting by **Mobeen Fazal**

Publishing consultation by **Sabrina von Nessen**

ISBN (Paperback): 979-8-9995055-0-7

7831 Wilson Farm Rd, Summerfield, NC 27358, USA

www.ingramcontent.com/pod-product-compliance
Lightning Source LLC
Chambersburg PA
CBHW031525120626
46545CB00005B/2007